I0803985

IMAGES
of America

BUFFALO ART DECO

Considered one of Buffalo's Art Deco masterpieces, Central Terminal is located just a little over two miles away from downtown at 495 Paderewski Drive. It is pictured here in about 1925. (Collection of the Buffalo History Museum. General photograph collection, Buildings–Transportation & Storage–Depots.)

IMAGES
of America

BUFFALO ART DECO

Trisha Charles

ARCADIA PUBLISHING

Copyright © 2023 by Trisha Charles
ISBN 978-1-4671-0743-3

Published by Arcadia Publishing
Charleston, South Carolina

Printed in the United States of America

Library of Congress Control Number: 2023930779

For all general information, please contact Arcadia Publishing:
Telephone 843-853-2070
Fax 843-853-0044
E-mail sales@arcadiapublishing.com
For customer service and orders:
Toll-Free 1-888-313-2665

Visit us on the Internet at www.arcadiapublishing.com

Contents

Acknowledgments		6
Introduction		7
1.	City Hall	9
2.	Transportation	31
3.	Industry and Commerce	53
4.	Broadcasting and Newspapers	65
5.	Nightlife and Entertainment	79
6.	Education	89

Acknowledgments

There are so many Buffalonians to thank in the creation of this book, many of whom wondered if it would make it to publication. Starting this project at the beginning of the COVID pandemic brought about challenges I could not have foreseen or prepared for. I would like to thank all those who provided continued support in my research endeavors: Cynthia Vaness at the Buffalo Historic Society for her guidance and research expertise; Peter Savage Sr. for his time and infinite wisdom on city hall; and Daniel DiLandro, from the E.H. Butler Library at Buffalo State College, for his assistance and direction. My gratitude and thanks to Cheryl Belczak and Chuck LaChiusa for their kindness in providing their time, photography, and talent—their generosity helped to make this possible. Thank you, Stacia Bannerman at Arcadia, for pushing me and driving this project to the end.

And to my family and friends, thank you for your love and support. Most importantly, a special thanks to my daughter for her inspiration and curiosity and my husband for his patience and understanding. Much love to all.

INTRODUCTION

Several movements helped to define the era known as the Roaring Twenties. Prohibition brought about the speakeasy, moonshine, and the flapper along with the arrival of the Jazz Age and Art Deco. The styling of the Art Deco movement influenced everything from fashion to interior design, graphic design, the movie industry, the automobile industry, and architecture. The architectural style of Art Deco first appeared in Paris from 1903 to 1904 in two apartment complexes by Auguste Perret and Henri Sauvage. The residence utilized reinforced concrete, which is a process of adding steel mesh, bars, or rods to concrete to make it stronger. This process allowed for taller buildings to be developed, and the skyscraper would change modern city skylines.

It would be 1925 before the movement was officially introduced at the Exposition of Modern Decorative and Industrial Arts in Paris. Also called Moderne, Art Deco attempted to bridge early modern European architecture with fine art and commercial trends. The term *Art Deco* was not widely used to describe the styling until the 1960s, when art historian and critic Bevis Hillier used it in his book *Art Deco of the 20s and 30s*. With inspiration from several other artistic movements, including Cubism, Futurism, Fauvism, and Constructivism, the Art Deco movement would replace Art Nouveau. Geometric shapes and bold rich colors are used instead of flowing curvy lines and muted color palettes. Art Deco is also purely decorative, unlike Art Nouveau, which has a philosophical approach.

Art Deco was predominantly used for commercial buildings of hotels and retail, government buildings, train stations, theaters, high-rise offices, and apartment buildings. The exteriors characteristically utilized reinforced concrete, straight lines, symmetry, sharp angles, chevrons, and zigzags. A variety of materials like stucco, terra-cotta, decorative glass, chrome, steel, and aluminum were also incorporated into the designs. Rarely would it be seen in the design of new homes, but occasionally, Art Deco elements would be added to preexisting houses. The interiors of Art Deco buildings were vibrant and bright, adorned with sculptures, murals, and intricate floor and ceiling patterns made from glass, marble, ceramic and stainless steel. Color palettes were bright and deep yellows, reds, greens, blues, and pinks combined with black and white, silver, and gold to create high contrast. In addition to the Cubism and Futurism inspiration, Ancient Egyptian, Greco-Roman, and Mesoamerican architecture played a role in the modern designs. When King Tut's tomb was discovered in 1922, it would bring a revival of Egyptian patterns and designs. Art Deco represented luxury and glamor, a modern trend that was fast and forward-thinking. Beyond architecture, the movement influenced jewelry, fashion, art, and furniture. Women's fashion became more masculine with sleeker, streamlined silhouettes, shorter skirts, and shorter haircuts. Furniture utilized exotic woods, jewel-tone colors, lacquer finishes, mirrored surfaces, and shiny metals.

During this time, Buffalo was a thriving city experiencing a period of growth. The positioning of the city on the Great Lakes provided a critical location. With the force of Niagara Falls, hydroelectric power was utilized and Buffalo was the first American city to have widespread electric light, hence the nickname "City of Light." The Pan-American Exposition in 1901 celebrated the city as a leading center in industry, commerce, and culture, which attracted a number of industries to the region. The city's many waterways also allowed goods to be transported. Large companies like Bethlehem Steel, Pierce-Arrow Company, Larkin Company, and the Curtiss Aeroplane and Motor Company created thousands of jobs. The significance the economic boom had on the city led to investments in the arts. The Buffalo and Erie County Historical Museum opened in one of the buildings left behind by the Pan-American Exposition. In 1905, the Albright Knox Art Gallery opened, and jazz musicians from all over the world were coming to Buffalo to play at the Colored Musicians Club. With the increase in population and the belief the growth trend would continue, Buffalo built one of the finest examples of Art Deco: Central Terminal.

But the momentum that Art Deco had during 1920–1930 came to an end with the crash of the stock market in 1929. Designs became less ornate and mass-produced. With the emergence of World War II, metals needed to be used to build arms and were no longer used for decorative arts. The decadence and glamor of Art Deco styling also seemed inappropriate during such a low point in history. While the style of architecture was still used until 1945, it changed with the addition of rounded edges and long flat lines. This new type of Art Deco architecture was called Streamline Moderne and had more horizontal focus than vertical. It occasionally utilized nautical themes featuring portholes and handrails that evoked the feeling of a ship.

Between 1940 and 1950, Buffalo continued to grow with the population peaking at 580,132, according to the census of 1950. Much of this growth came from the African American population migrating from the rural south to the northern cities to obtain employment. While those who could afford to commute opted to leave the city for the suburbs, historical buildings were demolished and replaced with parking lots. Automobile and air travel replaced the need for trains and the once-grand Central Terminal shut down in 1979. Unfortunately, the terminal has been vacant for the better part of 30 years and is not currently open to the public. But with the resurgence of the city and the dedication of the Central Terminal Restoration Group, the redevelopment of the terminal is underway with plans to create a center for events, tourism, and cultural exchange. While other Art Deco buildings have been demolished throughout the years, Buffalo is still rich with examples from the Roaring Twenties. Art Deco gems like city hall, the Courier-Express Building, and the Rand are still in use, and city hall even provides tours to the public several times a week.

One

City Hall

The pride of Buffalo's Art Deco architecture, city hall, sits at 65 Niagara Square, rising 32 stories, 398 feet high from the ground to the top of the tower. It was built between 1929 and 1930 by John W. Cowper Company for a total of $6,851,547 plus $400,000 in architectural fees. The building was completed for occupancy on November 10, 1931. In July 1932, as part of the 100th anniversary of Buffalo's incorporation as a city, the building was officially dedicated and open to the public. (Library of Congress, Prints & Photographs Division, HABS NY, 15-BUF, 13-.)

On September 16, 1929, the ground was broken for city hall on the site of the Wilkeson Mansion, home of Sam Wilkeson, who was appointed Buffalo's fifth mayor from 1836 to 1837. The home was built in 1824. (Collection of the Buffalo History Museum. General photograph collection, Buildings-Residences-Private.)

Sam Wilkeson would be known as the builder of Buffalo when he led the effort to construct a harbor in Buffalo. This made Buffalo the western terminal of the Erie Canal instead of Black Rock, which was a smaller village but had a natural harbor. (Collection of the Buffalo History Museum. General photograph collection, Persons-W.)

The Wilkeson residence was initially demolished in 1915 and replaced with Buffalo's first gas station before it was made the site for city hall. By design, the columns of city hall would line up with the columns of the Wilkeson Mansion. (Collection of the Buffalo History Museum. General photograph collection, Buildings-Residences-Private.)

The step-back styling with dramatic vertical bans, a central tower, and 15-story wings is reminiscent of the Mayan pyramids and characteristic of Art Deco. The ziggurat, or a tower in the form of a terraced pyramid built by the ancient Assyrians and Babylonians, served as inspiration for many Art Deco buildings during this period. This form also solved a design challenge created by the 1916 Zoning Resolution in New York City. It would be the first citywide zoning code in the United States and required sunlight to reach the ground unobstructed by massive buildings. (Collection of the Buffalo History Museum. General photograph collection, Buildings-Government.)

The exterior of the octagonal tower is rich with colorful red and yellow patterns and topped with a glass dome, which sits just above the crown. Large sculpted eagles with wings spread accentuate each corner of the octagon. The base of the dome consists of brightly colored triangular tiles combining to form larger triangular chevrons giving the appearance of a crown. Elevators are prevented from reaching beyond the 25th floor due to the narrowness of the upper part of the tower. However, by climbing the stairs up to the 28th floor, one can visit the observation deck. The public has a breathtaking 365-degree view of the city from a narrow exterior gallery. (Left, photograph by Cheryl Belczak; below, Library of Congress, Prints & Photographs Division, HABS NY, 15-BUF, 13–.)

This photograph from 1931 shows the interior of the glass dome and exterior of the tower illuminated at night. At the time, 369 floodlights would illuminate the building from dusk until dawn. Today, the dome can be lit to reflect and celebrate holidays, sports teams, charities, corporations, and various causes and events. (Collection of the Buffalo History Museum. General photograph collection, Buildings–Government.)

With a constant background of water and sky, city hall has a dramatic presence at Niagara Square, which is positioned at the geographical center of the city. Joseph Ellicott who assisted his brother on the radial street plan for Washington, DC, developed a similar concept for Buffalo in 1804. Niagara Square, which is now a circular space, was once a large open intersection of eight streets. (Library of Congress, Prints & Photographs Division, HABS NY, 15-BUFF, 13-.)

From September 28 to November 23, 1930, there was noticeable progress made in the construction of the building. These two images highlight the number of windows. From the first floor to the 25th, there are 1,520 windows. A unique design feature allows for the windows to open inward eliminating the need for window washers. It takes only 10 days to clean the windows of the entire building. (Both, Library of Congress, Prints & Photographs Division, HABS NY, 15-BUFF, 13-.)

The monument in front of city hall was erected in 1907 to commemorate Pres. William McKinley, who was assassinated in Buffalo in 1901 while attending the Pan-American Exposition. The obelisk monument is made of Vermont and Italian marble. The four lions surrounding the base represent strength, and the turtles symbolize immortality. (Library of Congress, Prints & Photographs Division, HABS NY, 15-BUFF, 13-.)

Men are pictured here laying the cornerstone on May 14, 1930. It would be another year and a half before the building would be completed. In July 1932, it was dedicated. (Collection of the Buffalo History Museum. General photograph collection, Buildings–Government.)

In 1926, the city architect's designs for city hall were rejected, and the common council turned to John J. Wade (standing on the left), who would serve as the chief architect of the building. At this time, Wade had partnered with George J. Dietal to form the architectural firm Dietal & Wade, which would design city hall. With John Cowper as general contractor and Wade as the architect, the duo completed other projects in Buffalo during this period, including the Rand Building, which is highlighted later in this book. (Collection of the Buffalo History Museum. General photography collection, Buildings–Government.)

Eight columns support a sculptural sandstone frieze at the front entrance of the building. The frieze is over 11 feet high and nearly 100 feet long. The sculptor, Albert T. Stewart, collaborated on the design with John J. Wade, the architect. (Library of Congress, Prints & Photographs Division, HABS NY, 15-BUFF, 13-.)

The back entrance, or West elevation frieze, was also sculpted by Stewart and portrays scenes from the early history of Buffalo. The scenes are shown in chronological order and date from 1758 to 1825. The center scene of 1810 shows representatives of the Iroquois people meeting in council. Red Jacket, the Seneca Orator presents a tomahawk to the Native American Agent Erastus Granger. The actual tomahawk is currently in the collection of the Buffalo & Erie County Historical Society. (Library of Congress, Prints & Photographs Division, HABS NY, 15-BUFF, 13-.)

The East elevation depicts a sitting woman in the center, representing Buffalo's historian; with pen and book, she is ready to write the events of the next century. The balanced groups of figures on either side of her represent the people of Buffalo, both past and present. To the right are the people of former generations passing knowledge and guidance, and to the left are people of the modern city of Buffalo. (Both, Library of Congress, Prints & Photographs Division, HABS NY, 15-BUFF, 13-.)

Upon entering the building, the three-story barrel-vaulted ceiling of the main lobby is decorated in intricate patterns of colorful tile set between decorative bands of stone. The Akoustolith painted tiles made of a porous ceramic material limits the noise in large vaulted areas. The tiles were installed by the Rafael Guastavino Co. Their patented tiling system was based on the traditional building methods behind Catalan Vaulting. The system's structural form also provided fireproof properties. (Library of Congress, Prints & Photographs Division, HABS NY, 15-BUFF, 13-.)

The decorated tiles with painted panels outline the octagon in the center of the ceiling. This repeating pattern is representative of the octagon tower that stretches 28 stories above. (Both, (Library of Congress, Prints & Photographs Division, HABS NY, 15-BUFF, 13-.)

The front and rear entrances of the lobby display large murals painted by William de Leftwich Dodge. The above mural titled "Talents Diversified Find Vent in Myriad Form" represents all of Buffalo's industries from agriculture to water commerce, steel making, and transportation. The image below of "Frontiers Unfettered by Any Frowning Fortress" shows the significance of Buffalo's proximity to the Canadian border. The central female figure, representing Buffalo, holds the United States to the left and Canada to the right. (Both, Library of Congress, Prints & Photographs Division, HABS NY, 15-BUFF, 13-.)

In the main lobby stand four marble statues, two female and two male. Each statue is representative of character traits that are expected of good citizens: virtue, diligence, service, and fidelity. The figures were sculpted by Albert T. Stewart, the same sculptor of the friezes. The statue shown in this photograph is Fidelity. (Library of Congress, Prints & Photographs Division, HABS NY, 15-BUFF, 13-.)

A two-story vaulted corridor ends with a smaller Dodge mural, pictured here. There are an additional four smaller murals at the end of each corridor that represent Buffalo's public services. The lunettes are half-moon-shaped murals that represent charity, protection, education, and construction. (Library of Congress, Prints & Photographs Division, HABS NY, 15-BUFF, 13-.)

Located on the 13th floor, the common council chambers hold legislative branch meetings and public hearings. Meetings of the common council have happened since the building was completed every Tuesday afternoon. The room is constructed in a three-story semicircular amphitheater that seats 383 people. The public enters from the upper level following a circular gallery to the left and right. Seven concentric rows of seats descend from the gallery to the council floor. (Library of Congress, Prints & Photographs Division, HABS NY, 15-BUFF, 13-.)

The interior of the doorway is framed in brown marble and decorated with carvings of human faces and animals. Each of the faces symbolizes wisdom, strength, and authority while the animals represent loyalty of the dog, courage of the lion, forcefulness of the hawk, and self-sacrifice of the pelican. On either side of the middle doors are two wood carvings of tomahawks, sculpted by the Lippich Brothers of Lancaster, New York. (Photograph by Cheryl Belczak.)

Just above the semicircular seating is this ceiling of Guastavino acoustic tile, decorated with a variety of Native American motifs. (Library of Congress, Prints & Photographs Division, HABS NY, 15-BUFF, 13-.)

In the 1920s, the majority of men were still wearing hats. The hat holder found underneath the bottom of each seat, provided space for the men to store their hats during public meetings. (Photograph by Cheryl Belczak.)

On the wall behind the dais, there stands seven fluted columns made of French limestone. The columns are separated by tinted glass windows outlined with bronze grillwork. The inscription above on the colonnade reads, "The People's Councillors Reflect The People's Will." (Photograph by Cheryl Belczak.)

The semicircular stained glass is literally a skylight representing the heavens above. Continuing the geometric pattern of the seating, the glass has been constructed in seven concentric circles. The use of prismatic glass diffuses the light in such a way that no shadows are cast anywhere in the room. (Photograph by Cheryl Belczak.)

From the center of the skylight, a sunburst of red and yellow sun rays extends outward through the blue. John Wade likely had a hand in the design of the skylight, as there is a similarity to another sunburst design found in the Masonic Consistory on Delaware Avenue, which is now the auditorium and foyer of Canisius High School. (Library of Congress, Prints & Photographs Division, HABS NY, 15-BUFF, 13-.)

Two

TRANSPORTATION

The 17-story octagonal tower is made of buff-colored brick and stands 271 feet above track level. The top edge of the tower is outlined with sandstone volutes, or spiral scrolls that are characteristic of Ionic capitals. Extending from the terminal proper are two wings—one over the train concourse and the other a mail and baggage building. (Collection of the Buffalo History Museum. General photograph collection, Buildings-Transportation & Storage-Depots.)

Construction on Central Terminal started in 1927 at 495 Paderewski Drive. Designed for a growing city with a projected population of approximately 1.5 million, Central Terminal was built to handle a daily schedule of 200 trains, 10,000 passengers, and 1,500 employees. The station included shops, a restaurant, a soda fountain, and a parking garage. It was completed in 1929 for a total of $14 million, just months before the Great Depression began. (Collection of the Buffalo History Museum. General photograph collection, Buildings–Transportation & Storage–Depots–New York Central–Construction.)

Frank X. Schwab, seated in the center, was the mayor of Buffalo from 1922 to 1929. He was an unlikely candidate for mayor, as his career had been in the brewing industry. When Prohibition was enacted in 1919, Schwab transitioned into the production of near beer. However, when federal agents raided the Buffalo Brewing Company, Schwab's brewery, they discovered illegal beer, resulting in an indictment for Schwab. As a joke, in 1921, the Knights of St. John petitioned for his mayoral candidacy. On November 8, 1921, he was elected mayor. His career in politics would prove to be beneficial to the transportation industries in Buffalo. Not only was he instrumental in getting Central Terminal built, but he would also lay the cornerstone for the administration building of the Buffalo Airport. (Collection of the Buffalo History Museum. General photograph collection, Persons–S.)

Despite the city's speculation about the need for such a massive building, planning for Central Terminal began in 1924. An agreement would be signed in 1925 and The New York Central Railroad would build a central station in Buffalo to help relieve some of the congestion from the smaller city stations. The president of New York Central Railroad, Patrick Crowley, chose Alfred T. Fellheimer and Stewart Wagner to design the building. A controversial decision for the location of the new train station would put it 2.2 miles from the business center of the city. The location would surely accommodate a growing city. However, Buffalo's population would peak in 1950 at only 500,000, and the building would quickly become obsolete. (Photographs in the Carol M. Highsmith Archive, Library of Congress, Prints & Photographs Division.)

The grand opening was celebrated on June 22, 1929, with a chamber of commerce luncheon at noon for 2,200 people. Speakers for the event would include Henry Thornton, chairman of the board and president of the Canadian National Railways, and Frank X. Schwab, mayor of Buffalo. The Statler Hotel with support from other hotels would cater the largest event ever held in Buffalo, up to this point. At 2:00 p.m., the ceremonial train left the station bound for New York City, and the station officially opened when the celebration ended at 3:30 p.m. (Above, Collection of the Buffalo History Museum. Goldome/Nagle photograph collection, Picture G65, Buildings-Transportation & Storage-Depots; below, Collection of the Buffalo History Museum. General photograph collection, Buildings-Transportation & Storage-Depots.)

While much of the city of Buffalo is flat, travelers arriving at the station get the impression they are moving toward the rising ground. The curved incline combined with the circular plaza creates the illusion. Clocks were strategically placed at the four corners of the tower so that approaching travelers would know the correct time upon entering the terminal. (Collection of the Buffalo History Museum. General photograph collection, Buildings-Transportation & Storage-Depots.)

The main entrances at the base of the tower were marked with low-hanging marquees surrounded by large windows, as pictured here. At either end of the marquee, there are icons of train wheels with wings representing the new, fast, and graceful era of train travel. (Collection of the Buffalo History Museum. General photograph collection, Buildings-Transportation & Storage-Depots.)

The train concourse measured 50 feet wide by 450 feet long with seven platforms each serving two tracks. Under the 14 tracks was a baggage subway that extended 660 feet out from the main building. (Collection of the Buffalo History Museum. General photograph collection, Buildings-Transportation & Storage-Depots.)

Pictured here in 1954, during the railroad fair week, American Car & Foundry Talgo train was one of the first of the postwar lightweight streamliners. The hope was that these newly designed trains would bring a refreshed enthusiasm back to railroad travel. (Collection of the Buffalo History Museum. General photograph collection, Buildings-Transportation & Storage-Depots.)

At 271 feet high, the octagonal tower dominates the East Side skyline. Floodlights illuminating the tower at night made the building visible from a 15-mile radius. (Collection of the Buffalo History Museum. General photograph collection, Buildings-Transportation & Storage-Depots.)

The grand concourse with 15,000 square feet of space, has 60-foot vaulted ceilings made of Guastavino tiles. These terra-cotta tiles are standardized and are usually set in a herringbone pattern. Beyond the aesthetic appeal, the tiles solved the acoustical problems caused by the large openness of the space and the movement of the trains and people. The foundation pillars were also set on "vibration mats" that consisted of asbestos and lead. A system created by the New York Central Railroad in building Grand Central Station in New York City. To further help insulate the floor against the sound and vibration of the trains, the concrete floor base has a lining of cork two inches thick. The floor design is a terrazzo of marble in four colors: Cedar Tennessee, Pink Tennessee, Botticino (a dark gray marble imported from Italy), and Red Verona. (Collection of the Buffalo History Museum. General photograph collection, Buildings–Transportation & Storage–Depots.)

The Art Deco details of the interior, include metal and frosted-glass sconces, metal finials in fleur-de-lis patterns atop pilasters border the 18 ticket windows. Metal grillwork in geometric patterns and glamorous light fixtures placed at either end of the concourse. (Collection of the Buffalo History Museum. General photograph collection, Buildings–Transportation & Storage–Depots.)

The 450-foot-long concourse had 14 passenger tracks. The seven stairways to the outbound passengers' right each had a bulletin board with the departure time and destination of the train. Arriving travelers would use the seven openings to the left. These utilized ramps to make it easier for the arriving passengers to reach the concourse. Pictured here, the bustling main concourse is filled with travelers. (Collection of the Buffalo History Museum. General photograph collection, Buildings–Transportation & Storage–Depots.)

Next to the baggage check room, 18 ticket windows featuring ornate bronze grillwork extend across the west end of the concourse. Just above the ticket booths behind the decorative balustrade is a balcony. Near the center of the concourse, directly opposite of the ticket windows, is an information booth made of marble and bronze. (Collection of the Buffalo History Museum. General photograph collection, Buildings–Transportation & Storage–Depots.)

The Central Terminal clock featured a glass globe that when lit green was a silent signal to police in case of an incident. Similar to the Grand Central Station golden clock, the central information booth housed the four-sided clock in Central Terminal. In 2009, in honor of the terminal's 80th birthday, the clock was officially returned permanently to the main concourse. It had been purchased and restored in 2004 with $25,000 in support from M&T bank. As seen in this photograph, the original also included a newsstand that sold comforts, necessities, and luxuries to travelers. (Collection of the Buffalo History Museum. General photograph collection, Buildings–Transportation & Storage–Depots.)

The American bison that stands at the eastern end of the concourse was a subtle reminder of what city the incoming travelers were visiting. The original bison, or "Stuffy," as he was called, was actually a bison skin mounted on a frame of fine wire and papier-mache. Stuffy was a favorite as departing World War II soldiers would pull hair from the form for good luck. For over 30 years, the buffalo stood in the concourse waiting to be replaced with a bronze statue. When the terminal was abandoned, there was a period of vandalism, and Stuffy was destroyed. But in the early 1990s, the original artist mold was located by the University of Buffalo and a bronze version now stands in front of Alumni Arena. (Collection of the Buffalo History Museum. General photograph collection, Buildings–Transportation & Storage–Depots.)

Seen here is a view of the Gateway Restaurant's neon sign and the remodeled ticket windows. Neon signs became popular in 1923 when Georges Claude introduced his neon signs to a Packard Car dealership. The signs caught on quickly and were used in outdoor advertising throughout the United States. The Flexlume Sign Company, located in Buffalo, has been in business for over 100 years and employed 500 employees despite the Great Depression. (Collection of the Buffalo History Museum. General photograph collection, Buildings-Transportation & Storage-Depots-New York Central—Ticket Windows.)

The combination coffee shop/dining restaurant was located on the north side of the passenger concourse and could seat 250 people. The lunch counter was centered on a rounded W-shape with reflective black Carrara glass countertops. Black and gold marble lined the walls and silver and bronze grillwork formed dividers between the three sections. This area was the peak of the terminal's Art Deco interior. (Collection of the Buffalo History Museum. General photograph collection, Buildings-Transportation & Storage-Depots.)

Just off the main concourse is a waiting room with high back benches and seats on either side of the backrest. The walls and the ceiling are Spanish stucco, a contrast to the rest of the building. The painted ceiling overhead is of blue sky and clouds creating a feeling of the outdoors. Lights are set in the curved arch and four bas-relief medallions hang in the corners of the wall. Each medallion is a scene from New York State and includes the Statue of Liberty, West Point, Niagara Falls, and a New York City Hudson line locomotive. (Collection of the Buffalo History Museum. General photograph collection, Buildings–Transportation & Storage–Depots.)

Following World War II, when the popularity of air travel and automobiles increased, passenger train travel suffered. In 1955, the New York Central Railroad put Buffalo Central Terminal (BCT) up for sale. On October 28, 1979, the last train left Central Terminal. Finally, in August 1997, BCT property was transferred to Central Terminal Restoration Corporation (CTRC). Recently, the CTRC was awarded $61 million through the Regional Revitalization Partnership, a public and philanthropic initiative to bring economic growth to Buffalo's east side. (Photographs in the Carol M. Highsmith Archive, Library of Congress, Prints & Photographs Division.)

Pierce-Arrow, known for its line of luxury automobiles, debuted at the Pan-American Exhibition in 1901. The factory pictured above, located on Elmwood Avenue, is now a commerce park. George N. Pierce, who had achieved success in manufacturing bicycles for children and then adults, was producing some of the biggest and most expensive automobiles in the United States by 1905. In 1907, the Pierce-Arrow Motor Car Co. was officially launched. (Above, collection of the Buffalo History Museum. Goldome/Nagle photograph collection, Picture G65, Buildings–Factories–Automobile; right, collection of the Buffalo History Museum. General photography collection, Persons–Pierce.)

Pierce would be known for a number of automotive innovations, but the most notable and distinctive was the fender light designed by Herbert Dawley in 1914. Dawley also designed the hood ornament known as the "Helmeted Archer" used on the 1928 Pierce-Arrow. The hood ornament design can be seen here in an advertisement from 1937. (Collection of the Buffalo History Museum. Vertical file: Manufacturing.)

In 1928, Pierce-Arrow was purchased by Studebaker Corporation and a second showroom would be built at the intersection of Main Street and Jewett Avenue. It was designed with Art Deco styling by H.E. Plumer and Associates in conjunction with Harold F. Kellogg and was intended to be the prototype for all Pierce-Arrow showrooms around the United States. The exterior of the building greets the customer with brass double doors at the front of the building. Terra-cotta is used throughout the detail of the volutes and molding at the top of the tower and edge of the building. (Collection of the Buffalo History Museum. General photograph collection, Buildings–Business & Commercial–Auto Dealers–Pierce–Arrow.)

Much of the original interior of the showroom at 2421 Main Street has been preserved and features Art Deco designs of frosted sconces and light fixtures. Marble, brass, and backlit art glass frame the doorway. The decorative sunken panels or coffered ceiling features Pierce-Arrow wheel decorations in each corner. Unfortunately, the auto industry would be hit hard with the onset of the Great Depression, and Studebaker went bankrupt in 1933 and sold Pierce-Arrow to Buffalo Management. In 1999, Greater Buffalo Savings purchased the building, saving it from destruction, and began restorations in 2002. The building is currently a branch of Key Bank. (Collection of the Buffalo History Museum. General photograph collection, Buildings–Business & Commercial–Auto Dealers–Pierce–Arrow.)

Studebaker invested money in research and new developments for Pierce-Arrow, which resulted in changes to the engineering and design of the cars. Roadsters, touring cars, and sedans were longer than previous models and sat lower to the ground. The Pierce Silver Arrow sedan was a concept car launched in 1933 at the New York City Auto Show. The Art Deco car was stylized with swooping fenders, a long hood, and highly streamlined shapes. (Both, Collection of the Buffalo History Museum. General photograph collection, Transportation-Land Auto.)

Depicted in the lower left of this photograph is a painting by Will Foster for Pierce-Arrow in 1912. The larger painting above of a similar scene shows the differences in the design of the car and women's fashions 18 years later in 1930. The front of the automobile was stretched out providing a longer, leaner-looking vehicle, and three years later, the lines are even softer with the introduction of the sedan. (Author's collection.)

Three

INDUSTRY AND COMMERCE

The former Mabel Danahy Building was designed by Duane Lyman in the late 1920s. Today, 443 Delaware Avenue is called the Buffalo Design Collaborative. It was the original location of Danahy's, a high-end fashion boutique that catered to a stylish group of customers known as the carriage trade. Mabel Danahy and her sister founded the company in 1925. Along the top of the building, the repeating geometric scrolls are reminiscent of a sunburst. Two geometric-styled pilasters divide the bays. (Photograph by Chuck LaChiusa.)

A number of Art Deco elements adorn the entrance to the building. Directly over the door is a carved bas-relief of a geometric fountain with a sunburst in the background. Even the numbering of the address is a typical font of the era. Volutes, or scrolls, frame the top of the doorway. (Both photographs by Chuck LaChiusa.)

This is a detail of one of the building sconces that sits above the north entrance of the building. The volute pattern is repeated in metal with frosted glass. (Photograph by Chuck LaChiusa.)

Framing the entrance to the right and left are decorative panels with repetitive patterns of scrolls and sun rays. This is a detail view of the right stone bas-relief. (Photograph by Chuck LaChiusa.)

The original exterior design of the Electric Building located at 20 East Huron Street, was built in the Beaux Arts Classical Revival style and was headquarters for Buffalo General Electric Company. It was designed by James A. Johnson and built in 1912. The building stands 14 stories high with a white-glazed terra-cotta exterior. (Collection of the Buffalo History Museum. General photograph collection, Buildings–Business & Commercial–Offices.)

The interior of the building was modified in the 1930s to a more Art Deco styling with the introduction of black ornamental glass, stainless steel, chrome trim, and ceiling medallions, and the tower was altered. At this time, the Buffalo Electric Company was consolidated into the Niagara Hudson Power Company. A full mezzanine floor was created with the elevator lobby, new entry vestibule, and interior walls treated in black structural glass and stainless steel trim. Pictured here, the building is decorated and lit for the Christmas holiday. Each year, the annual Buffalo Ball Drop on New Year's Eve is celebrated in Roosevelt Plaza as people gather to watch one of the largest ball drops outside of New York City. (Right, Collection of the Buffalo History Museum. General photograph collection, Buildings-Business & Commercial-Offices; below, the Courier-Express Photograph Collection, Archives & Special Collections Department, E.H. Butler Library, SUNY Buffalo State University.)

The Vars Building is located on the southwest corner of Delaware Avenue and West Chippewa Street. The four-story building was designed and planned by Addison Vars who named the building in memory of his father. It was built in 1929 by architects Lawrence Bley and Duane Lyman. A fine example of a commercial Art Deco building, its features include fluting along the top edge, pilasters with bas-relief Ionic capitals, and black fluted spandrel panels. (The Courier-Express Photograph & Special Collections Department, E.H. Butler Library, SUNY Buffalo State University.)

M.H. Birge was a wall-covering company started in 1834 by Martin H. Birge. George (pictured above) and Henry, Martin's sons, joined the company by 1875, and in August 1900, M.H. Birge & Sons was incorporated. They designed and developed high-end exclusive wallpapers until 1982, when the company shut down. (Collection of the Buffalo History Museum. General photograph collection, Persons–Birge.)

Martin Birge originally opened his dry goods store at 234 Main Street. The location of his business would change over the next 40 years due to growth, fire, and eventually, the shift from retail to manufacturing. Pictured here is the M.H. Birge wallpaper factory on Seventh Street at the corner of Maryland in 1886. (Collection of the Buffalo History Museum. Buffalo city directory, 1886, p. 121.)

It was calculated by the *Furniture Gazette* in 1849 that $8 million in wallpaper was sold in the United States at about 25¢ a roll. That same year, M.H. Birge & Sons started manufacturing wallpaper. By 1900, the country's production would increase to $100 million. This is the Birge factory in 1925, located at the corner of Niagara and Maryland Streets. (Collection of the Buffalo History Museum. Birge Collection, Mss. C77-02, Box 5, Folder 1.)

While the headquarters and the manufacturing warehouse were not designed in the Art Deco style, many of the wallpaper designs were inspired by E.A. Seguy, one of the most influential Art Deco designers. M.H. Birge promoted its employees as artisans practicing their art. Professional artists were hired to design papers. These images are wallpaper designs from 1920 to 1925. (Public domain.)

Charles Burchfield started as an assistant designer in 1921 working his way up to head of the department. This image is another example of wallpaper from the M.H. Birge factory. (Public domain.)

Lederman's Furniture Store at 239 Lombard Street is a four-story commercial building with Art Deco ornamentation. Built in 1929 by architect Louis Greenstein, who was also known for designing the city of Buffalo Flag and Erie County seal. The Art Deco lettering spells out the name of the company under a zigzagged pattern parapet. (Collection of the Buffalo History Museum. General photograph collection, Buildings–Business & Commercial–Furniture.)

Four

Broadcasting and Newspapers

Prior to 1924, two buildings stood at the corner of Lafayette Square and Main Street: the Olympic Theater and a restaurant called the Park Hof. The Marine Trust Company purchased the structures and then demolished them to build the Rand Building, which was completed in 1929 for $3 million. It was named for George F. Rand Sr., the former president and chairman of the board of directors of Marine Midland Bank. (Collection of the Buffalo History Museum. General photograph collection, Buildings–Business & Commercial Offices–Rand Building.)

James W. Kideney & Associates and Franklyn & William Kidd were the architectural firms that designed the Art Deco building at 14 Lafayette Square. John W. Cowper Co. Inc. constructed the 351-foot building. The neon beacon tower added another 40 feet, making it, at the time, the tallest building with 29 floors. It would remain the tallest skyscraper in Buffalo for 43 years. (Collection of the Buffalo History Museum. General photograph collection, Buildings–Business & Commercial–Offices–Rand Building.)

The granite base supports five stories of Indiana limestone and the remaining stories of buff brick. When the building was completed in 1929, it featured an elaborate lighting system, which highlighted the stepped-back Art Deco design of the building. It is said to have been the inspiration for the Empire State Building in New York City. The Rand Building would be more than an office and branch of the new Marine Midland Holding Company. It was designed to facilitate the high technology of the time, housing the main offices of Western Union and the studios of WGR radio. (Collection of the Buffalo History Museum. General photograph collection, Buildings-Business & Commercial-Offices-Rand Building.)

The Buffalo Broadcasting Company moved its stations WGR and WKBW to the building. The "GR" in WGR stands for George Rand. Today, the stations in the Townsquare Media Cluster broadcast from the studios in the Rand Building. It remains the second-tallest building in Buffalo. (Author's collection.)

In 1926, the *Buffalo Daily Courier* and the *Buffalo Morning Press* merged when the owner William James Connor decided to bring the two papers together at 785 Main Street and form the *Courier-Express*. Architects Monk & Johnson with H.D.A. Ganteaume utilized hollow-spun piling in the foundation of the building. The five-story building was only the second installation in the United States to use hollow spun concrete piles. This type of foundation is deep and transfers building loads further down from the surface. (Collection of the Buffalo History Museum. General photograph collection, Buildings–Business & Commercial–Newspapers.)

Construction of the Courier-Express Building started in 1930 as pictured here. The Courier-Express Building was completed in 1930 with Egyptian and Byzantine influences. Very typical of the Art Deco style, the exterior is decorated in artistic references to printing with the use of several symbols and words. The base of the five-story building is pink Vermont granite with a cream terra-cotta facade. (Collection of the Buffalo History Museum. General photograph collection, Buildings, Business & Commercial–Newspapers.)

William James "Fingy" Conners, was born poor in the Old First Ward section of Buffalo in 1857. He was nicknamed "Fingy" due to a missing thumb that was the result of a childhood accident. When he was only 19, his parents passed and left him a saloon/rooming house. With the purchase of a second saloon, he began building his fortune. As a self-made millionaire, Conners became a real-estate developer, owner of a paving company and brewery, and publisher. On October 29, 1929, he died at 72, never seeing the results of his plan for a modern printing plant. (Collection of the Buffalo History Museum. General photograph collection, Persons–Conners.)

In November 1930, the presses were running for the grand opening. The formal event had women dressed in their finest and accessorized with pearls, while men fashioned their tuxes. (Above, the Courier-Express Photograph Collection, Archives & Special Collections Department, E.H. Butler Library, SUNY Buffalo State University; below, Collection of the Buffalo History Museum. General photograph collection, Buildings–Business & Commercial–Newspapers.)

The symbols cast in bronze over the main entrance are ancient printers' symbols that date back to a time when printers used signs instead of their names. The symbols are seen repeated throughout the building, on the lobby floor and the elevator doors. (Collection of the Buffalo History Museum. General photograph collection, Buildings–Business & Commercial–Newspapers.)

The building is pictured at night with the symbols backlit. (The Courier-Express Photograph Collection, Archives & Special Collections Department, E.H. Butler Library, SUNY Buffalo State University.)

The Main Street front features a relief of figures that represent the production process of a newspaper: the editor, linotyper, compositor, diemaker, stereotyper, pressman, shipper, and reader. At the top of the building stand four statues that portray the pioneers in printing and journalism: Johannes Gutenberg, John Peter Zenger, Christophe Plantin, and Benjamin Franklin. (Both, the Courier-Express Photograph Collection, Archives & Special Collections Department, E.H. Butler Library, SUNY Buffalo State University.)

There is even a reminder of the First Amendment of the Constitution of the United States on the exterior of the building: "Congress shall make no law abridging the freedom of speech or of the press." (Both, the Courier-Express Photograph Collection, Archives & Special Collections Department, E.H. Butler Library, SUNY Buffalo State University.)

Upon entering the building patrons were greeted with this large mural painted by Charles Bigelow and Ernst Davenport. It would take six months for the pair to complete the 10.5-by-20-foot painting on the east wall. The mural depicts the growth of Buffalo from a tiny village on the banks of the Buffalo creek to a thriving city in 1930 with city hall directly in the middle of the painting. The right segment of the painting features the future of a growing dynamic city with skyscrapers to the heavens. Simultaneously, the mural shows the merger of the *Courier* and the *Express* paper. (Collection of the Buffalo History Museum. General photograph collection, Buildings–Business & Commercial–Newspapers.)

The mural would dominate the lobby of the building for 55 years. On September 19, 1982, the paper ceased and the building sat vacant. In April 1985, the Catholic Diocese of Buffalo took over the building for $900,000 and began extensive renovations. The mural was removed from the lobby in 1987, rolled up, and stored in the basement until efforts were made to repair and restore the painting. Currently, the mural is waiting for funds to first examine the condition and then additional funds for its restoration. (Collection of the Buffalo History Museum. General photograph collection, Buildings-Business & Commercial-Newspapers.)

The printer symbols can be seen here on the floor of the lobby and the elevator doors. The ironwork of the mezzanine was furnished by Eberl Iron Works Inc., a family-owned company still operating out of Buffalo, New York. (Collection of the Buffalo History Museum. General photograph collection, Buildings, Business & Commercial–Newspapers.)

Five

Nightlife and Entertainment

Chez Ami was one of the first supper clubs in the country. The original owner, Philip Amigone, owned the club until his death in 1965. The interior of the club was designed by C. Theodore Macheras, and by utilizing mirrors, indirect lighting, neon, and plush carpeting, he achieved a modern Art Deco look. Invented by Amigone, the first rotating bar was installed and took seven-and-a-half minutes to complete one rotation. (Author's collection.)

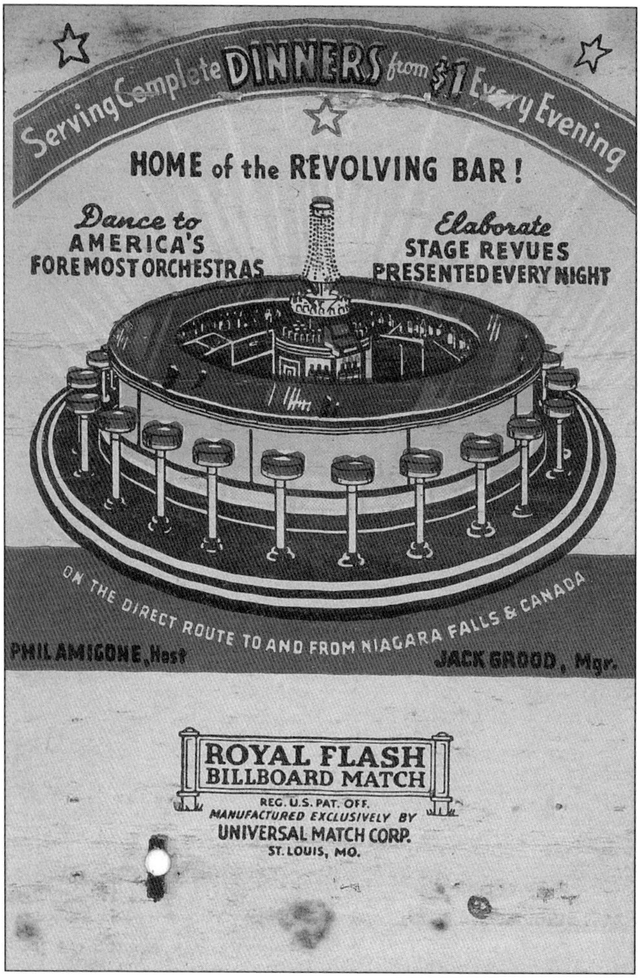

The Chez opened its doors in 1934 at 311 Delaware Avenue. The rotating bar was often used as the focal point for their advertising as noted on the matchbook covers shown here. In 1941, the Chez Ami suffered a fire that destroyed much of the interior. But by the spring of 1942, Chez reopened with a repaired revolving bar and much of the club's original Art Deco decor intact. (Both, author's collection.)

The Shea's Bailey Theater was designed by Henry and William Spahn and opened in 1928. By 1941, it was known as the Bailey Theater, an ornate Art Deco–styled theater. The interior of the theater, shown here, has strong linear lines with decorative ornate wallpaper. The theater could seat 1,790 patrons. The venue closed in 1977 and has since been demolished. (Collection of the Buffalo History Museum. General photograph collection, Buildings–Recreation–Theaters.)

Ellsworth M. Statler commissioned George B. Post & Sons to design a hotel at Delaware Avenue and Niagara Square. The 19-story Renaissance Revival Hotel Statler was completed in 1923. The supper menu shown here from January 15, 1924, features a dancing couple in an Art Deco styling. The illustration is simple with sleek and angular features of both the man and woman. The color palette is limited to yellow and blues with a strong use of black. (Collection of the Buffalo History Museum. Vertical file: Hotels & Motels–Statler.)

In 1910, Ann Montgomery owned the ice-cream parlor at 496 Michigan Avenue before converting it to an Oriental Billiard Parlor, and then to a supper club and hotel known as Little Harlem Hotel in 1929. While the exterior lacked the flair of Art Deco the atmosphere inside was certainly a sign of the times. (Collection of the Buffalo History Museum. General photography collection, Buildings–Refreshments–Saloons–Little Harlem.)

The Little Harlem Hotel and nightclub was placed on the list of national historic sites but unfortunately was destroyed by a fire in the 1990s. (Collection of the Buffalo History Museum. General photography collection, Buildings-Refreshments-Saloons-Little Harlem.)

The gayest spot in Buffalo had a splendid interior with draped ceilings, tinted walls, and an Oriental flair that was popular in the 1930s. The one-of-a-kind bandstand was designed by Ann Montgomery and was described as "a night in Wonderland." The club became a showcase for aspiring stars who otherwise would not have employment during an era when it was difficult for them to gain jobs in their professions. Among the star performers were Louis Armstrong, Billie Holiday, Bing Crosby, Vincent Lopez, Cab Calloway, and Dinah Washington. (Right, collection of the Buffalo History Museum Vertical File: Restaurants–Menus–Menu 1945; below, Collection of the Buffalo History Museum, General photograph collection, Buildings–Refreshments–Saloons.)

Ann Montgomery Woodson owned and operated the club in some capacity for 68 years. As one of the first female African American business owners in Buffalo, her club remained successful even through the Great Depression. Pictured above, Ann (standing) was married twice. Partnered in business and marriage, Ann divorced her first husband, Daniel Montgomery, in 1938. (Collection of the Buffalo History Museum. General photograph collection, Persons, M.)

Ann Montgomery married Paul Woodson sometime in the early 1940s. Pictured here with their bridal party, the newlyweds are in the back. Paul was a descendant of Pres. Thomas Jefferson and Sally Hemings, and before moving to Buffalo, he was stationed on the Tuskegee, Alabama, Air Force base. (Collection of the Buffalo History Museum. General photograph collection, Buildings-Refreshments-Saloons.)

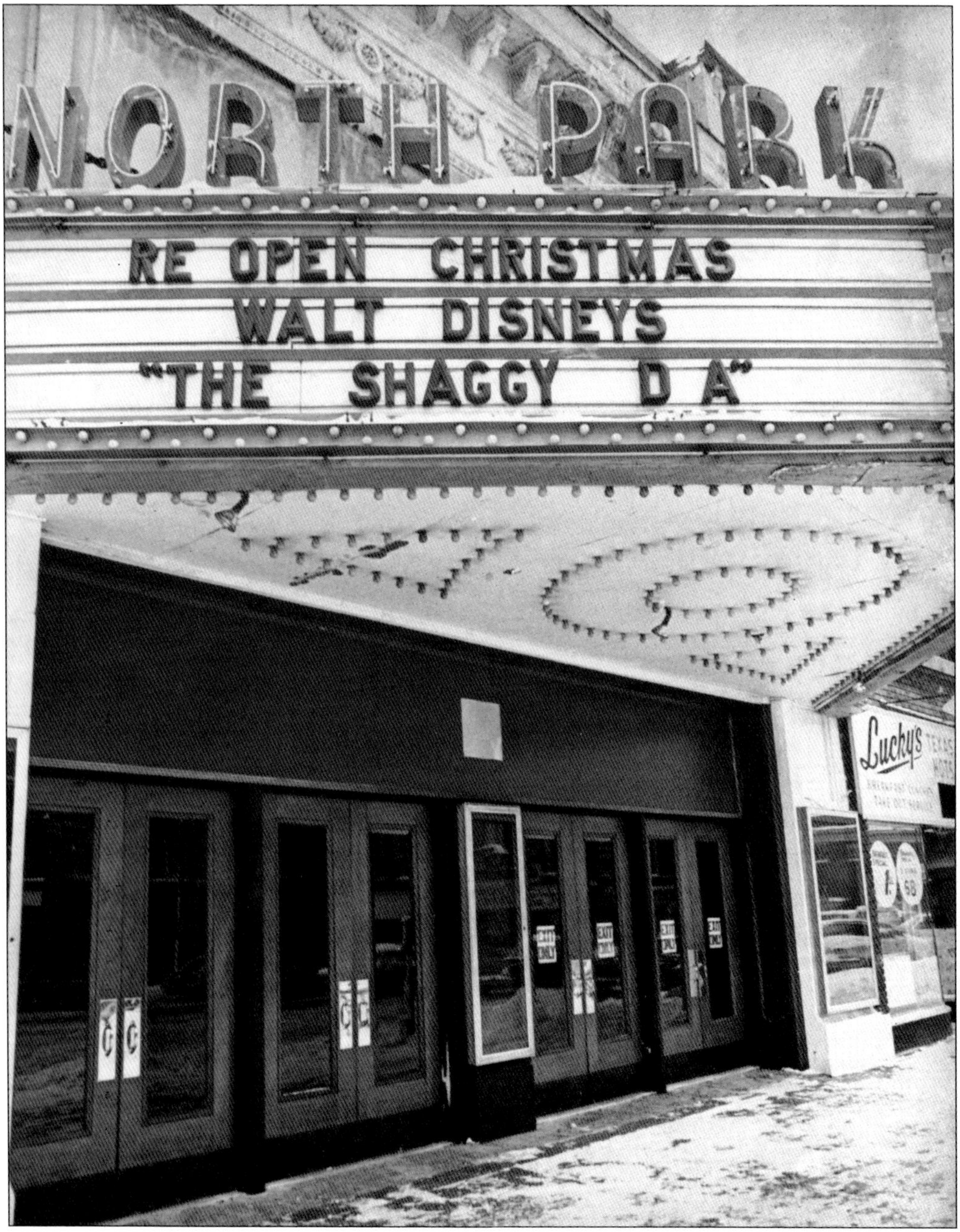

The North Park Theater opened on November 21, 1920. The foyer and auditorium are in the neoclassical style with six massive art nouveau murals painted by Raphael Beck. The iconic Art Deco marquee, seen here, came 20 years later in 1941. It was designed and built by Flexlume Signs, utilizing the popularity of neon. When Flexlume was called in 2014 to do restoration work, it was able to reference the original blueprints for the project. (The Courier-Express Photograph Collection, Archives & Special Collections Department, E.H. Butler Library, SUNY Buffalo State University.)

Six

EDUCATION

Kensington High School located at 319 Suffolk Street, was constructed in the 1930s and opened its doors in 1937. Architect Daniel G. McNeil designed the building, which was a project of the Federal Emergency Administration of Public Works. After 67 years in operation, the school closed in 2003 for a number of reasons, including financial challenges and poor academic performance. Renovations started in 2005, and in the fall of 2012, the school reopened as PS 64 Frederick Law Olmsted School. The school now operates as the gifted and talented program for the Buffalo Public Schools. (Photograph by Cheryl Belczak.)

The primary facade features a series of setbacks that create a stepped outline characteristic of Art Deco architecture. Strong vertical bands are used and emphasize an upward motion, drawing the eye to look up. (Photograph by Cheryl Belczak.)

The front entrance of the building is adorned with two stylized buffalo heads facing inward toward a central sunburst. Sunbursts are characteristic of Art Deco design and were used frequently in bas relief. The use of chevrons and zigzags are very distinctive geometrical details that are easily identifiable as Art Deco designs. (Photograph by Cheryl Belczak.)

The Common Bond (or American Bond) brick pattern has a header on every sixth row. This brickwork was commonly used as it could quickly be laid. The use of the geometrical eagle would seem to present a reminder of the school motto, which was "Aegis Fortissima Virtus," or "Virtue is the Strongest Shield." (Photograph by Cheryl Belczak.)

The Art Deco lettering indicates the entrance to the auditorium. The decorative repeat scallop and star patterns adorn the entrances with a decorative owl head that represents wisdom. (Photograph by Cheryl Belczak.)

Spandrel panels fill the space above the head of a window on one floor and, below, the sill of the window on the next floor. The black vertical bas-relief designs include men holding books and torches, which symbolize the enlightenment and hope of education. (Photograph by Cheryl Belczak.)

Burgard High School located at 400 Kensington Avenue was designed by Ernst Crimi in 1929. The building utilizes Art Deco design with Gothic Revival features to an industrial form. City Council designated $1 million in 1926 for the construction of a new facility to house the vocational school. Henry P. Burgard's five-acre donation to the city was made with the understanding the school would be named Burgard Vocational School. The cornerstone was laid on November 22, 1929, and the school opened in September 1930. The building could accommodate 1,500 students and had 47 classrooms and shop rooms, an auditorium, a double gymnasium, a library, and a cafeteria. The most unique feature of the school was a four-story automobile ramp, which was used to drive cars to the top-floor auto shops. The stage in the auditorium could exhibit automobiles with a 25-foot rear door opening to the auto shop. (Collection of the Buffalo History Museum. Hauser Bob Photograph Collection, Picture B63, Buildings–Educational–High Schools.)

The three-story school has a rectangular shape plan with a flat roof with a symmetrical front four-story center bay tower. There are thick vertical stone bands or mullions between the adjoining windows and vertical bands. The first floor is stone-faced with buff brick. (Collection of the Buffalo History Museum. General photograph collection, Buildings–Educational–High Schools.)

Discover Thousands of Local History Books Featuring Millions of Vintage Images

Arcadia Publishing, the leading local history publisher in the United States, is committed to making history accessible and meaningful through publishing books that celebrate and preserve the heritage of America's people and places.

Find more books like this at
www.arcadiapublishing.com

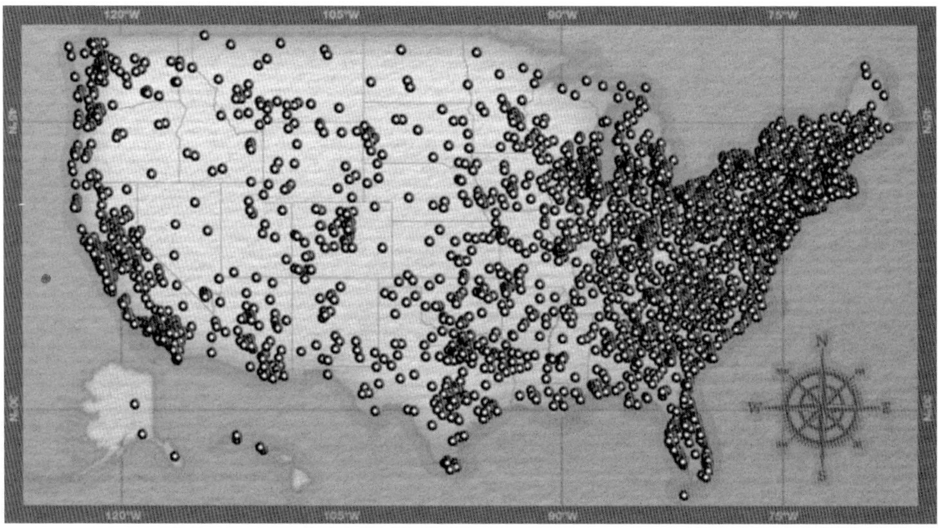

Search for your hometown history, your old stomping grounds, and even your favorite sports team.

Consistent with our mission to preserve history on a local level, this book was printed in South Carolina on American-made paper and manufactured entirely in the United States. Products carrying the accredited Forest Stewardship Council (FSC) label are printed on 100 percent FSC-certified paper.

MADE IN THE USA